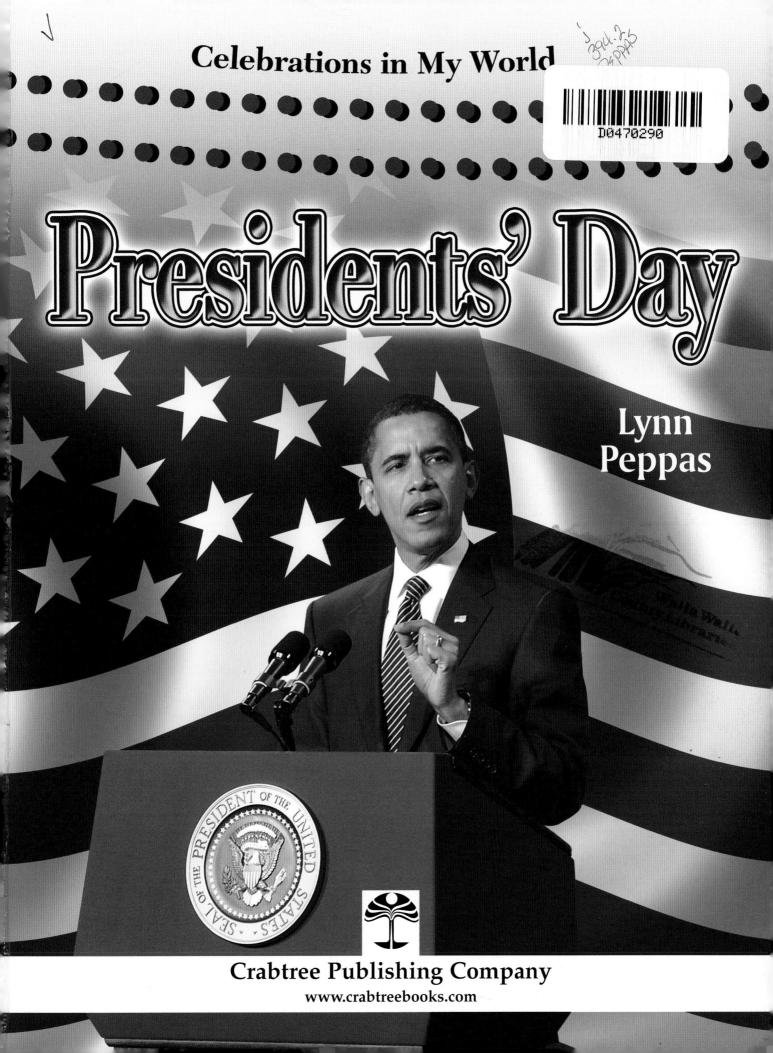

Celebrations in My World

Presidents' Day

Lynn Peppas

Crabtree Publishing Company

www.crabtreebooks.com

Crabtree Publishing Company

www.crabtreebooks.com

Author: Lynn Peppas
Coordinating editor: Chester Fisher
Series and project editor: Penny Dowdy
Editor: Adrianna Morganelli
Proofreader: Crystal Sikkens
Editorial director: Kathy Middleton
Production coordinator: Katherine Berti
Prepress technician: Katherine Berti
Project manager: Kumar Kunal (Q2AMEDIA)
Art direction: Dibakar Acharjee (Q2AMEDIA)
Cover design: Tarang Saggar (Q2AMEDIA)
Design: Neha Kaul (Q2AMEDIA)
Photo research: Farheen Aadil (Q2AMEDIA)

Photographs:
Alamy: Dennis MacDonald: p. 22; North Wind
    Picture Archives: p. 18, 24; Michael Ventura: p. 15
Associated Press: p. 10; Gino Domenico: p. 8;
    Eric Draper: p. 4
The Bridgeman Art Library: American School
    (19th century) Private Collection/Peter Newark
    American Pictures: p. 12
Corbis: Blue Lantern Studio: p. 16
Dreamstime: Buttershug: front cover (foreground);
    Richard Gunion: p. 9; Wayne Mckown: p. 23
Getty Images: Kean Collection: p. 17
Istockphoto: p. 20
loc.gov: p. 6, 7, 14, 21
Reuters: Jason Reed: p. 5
Shutterstock: Benjaminet: p. 11; Christopher Halloran:
    p. 1 (foreground); iofoto: front cover (background);
    Wendy Kaveney Photography: p. 29; Yegor Korzh:
    p. 26 (bottom); Philip Lange: p. 26 (top); Jonathan
    Larsen: p. 27; Lindsay Noechel: p. 30; Stephen
    Orsillo: p. 19; Carsten Reisinger: p. 1 (background);
    Christophe Testi: p. 28 (right); Brad Thompson: p. 31;
    Vladimir Wrangel: p. 28 (left); Andrey Yushkov: p. 13
Wikipedia: Dmadeo: p. 25

Library and Archives Canada Cataloguing in Publication

Peppas, Lynn
    Presidents' Day / Lynn Peppas.

(Celebrations in my world)
Includes index.
ISBN 978-0-7787-4756-7 (bound).--ISBN 978-0-7787-4774-1 (pbk.)

    1. Presidents' Day--Juvenile literature. 2. Presidents--United States--
History--Juvenile literature. I. Title. II. Series: Celebrations in my world

E176.8.P46 2010   j394.261   C2009-902111-0

Library of Congress Cataloging-in-Publication Data

Peppas, Lynn.
    Presidents' Day / Lynn Peppas.
        p. cm. -- (Celebrations in my world)
    Includes index.
    ISBN 978-0-7787-4774-1 (pbk. : alk. paper) -- ISBN 978-0-7787-4756-7
(reinforced library binding : alk. paper)
    1. Presidents' Day--Juvenile literature. 2. Presidents--United States--History--
Juvenile literature. I. Title.

    E176.8.P47 2010
    394.261--dc22
                                    2009014296

Crabtree Publishing Company

www.crabtreebooks.com   1-800-387-7650

Published in Canada
Crabtree Publishing
616 Welland Ave.
St. Catharines, ON
L2M 5V6

Published in the United States
Crabtree Publishing
PMB16A
350 Fifth Ave., Suite 3308
New York, NY 10118

Published in the United Kingdom
Crabtree Publishing
White Cross Mills
High Town, Lancaster
LA1 4XS

Published in Australia
Crabtree Publishing
386 Mt. Alexander Rd.
Ascot Vale (Melbourne)
VIC 3032

Contents

What is a President?

A president is a person who is chosen by the citizens of a country to run their government. The United States of America is a country in North America. Every four years Americans **elect**, or vote for, a president to lead their country.

President George W. Bush was the leader of the United States from 2001 to 2009.

DID YOU KNOW?

A president's term of office in the United States is four years. A person cannot be president for more than two terms, or eight years.

4

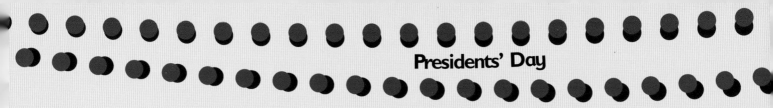

President Barack Obama is sworn into office in 2009 beside his wife, Michelle.

From 1776 to 2009, the United States has had 44 presidents in office. To become president in the United States, a person has to be a citizen that is 35 years of age or older, and has lived in the United States for at least 14 years.

What is Presidents' Day?

Presidents' Day is a **patriotic** holiday celebrated in the United States. Being patriotic means you love your country. Every year Presidents' Day is held on the third Monday in February.

George Washington's birthday was celebrated by Americans as far back as 1796.

DID YOU KNOW?

Americans living in the District of Columbia celebrated the first Presidents' Day as Washington's Birthday, on February 22, 1796.

On Presidents' Day, many Americans honor Abraham Lincoln.

On Presidents' Day, Americans honor all of the people who have been president of the United States, especially George Washington and Abraham Lincoln. Their leadership helped the United States become the country it is today.

What is a Federal Holiday?

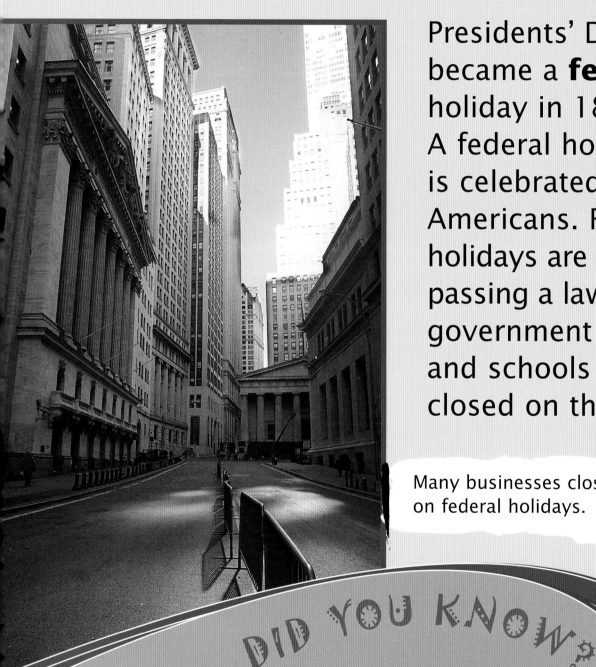

Presidents' Day became a **federal** holiday in 1885. A federal holiday is celebrated by all Americans. Federal holidays are made by passing a law. Banks, government offices, and schools are closed on this day.

Many businesses close on federal holidays.

DID YOU KNOW?

President George Washington was the first American president to have a federal holiday created to honor his birthday.

The Capitol building where **Congress** meets is closed on Presidents' Day.

Even though it is a holiday for every American, different states celebrate the holiday in different ways. Some call the holiday Washington's Birthday, or Washington-Lincoln Day. Some states celebrate it as Washington's Birthday only, and celebrate Lincoln's birthday as a state holiday on February 12.

Creating Presidents' Day

Washington's and Lincoln's birthdays were celebrated on February 22 until 1971. Congress made a new law called the Uniform Monday Holiday Act that stated certain holidays must fall on a Monday, creating three-day weekends.

Congress changed the dates of some holidays to always fall on Mondays.

DID YOU KNOW?

Congress never approved a name change of Washington's Birthday to Presidents' Day. As a federal holiday, it is still called Washington's Birthday.

● Today, Presidents' Day is always the third Monday in February.

February 2010

Mon	Tue	Wed	Thu	Fri	Sat	Sun
1	2	3	4	5	6	7
8	9	10	11	12	13	14
15	16	17	18	19	20	21
22	23	24	25	26	27	28

The law changed Washington's Birthday to the third Monday in February. At that time, a member of Congress suggested the name of the holiday also be changed to Presidents' Day. The suggestion was turned down, and the offical name is still Washington's Birthday.

Young George Washington

George Washington was born on February 22, 1732, in Wakefield, Virginia. He grew up on his family's farm where he learned how to ride a horse and hunt.

He studied at home with his father and older brother. His father died when he was eleven.

When George was a teenager he worked as a land **surveyor**.

As a young man, George became a skilled **military** leader. His soldiers respected him and thought he was brave and loyal.

Washington lived on this farm, called Mount Vernon.

DID YOU KNOW?

George Washington lived and worked on a large farm in Virginia called Mount Vernon. Today it is a historical museum that many people visit.

President George Washington

Before George Washington became president, America was a **colony** ruled by Britain. British colonists living in America wanted to form and rule their own country. A war called the American Revolution began between Britain and the colonists.

Washington led troops against the British in the American Revolution.

DID YOU KNOW?

The American Revolution lasted for eight years. It began in 1775 and ended in 1783.

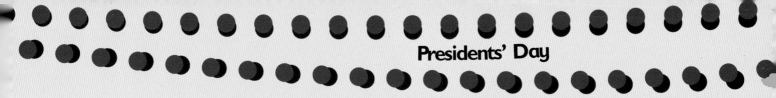

This display shows George Washington being sworn in as the first U.S. president.

Washington led the colonists' army to victory against the British army. The American colonies were able to create a free and **independent** country. Washington helped write the new country's Constitution, which is a list of people's freedoms and rights. He became the first president of the United States in 1789.

Young Abraham Lincoln

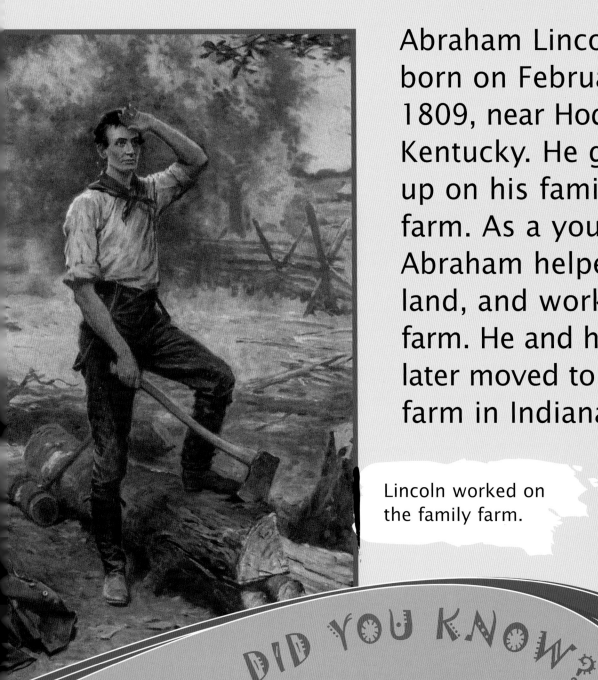

Abraham Lincoln was born on February 12, 1809, near Hodgenville, Kentucky. He grew up on his family's farm. As a young man Abraham helped clear land, and work the farm. He and his family later moved to another farm in Indiana.

Lincoln worked on the family farm.

DID YOU KNOW?

Abraham Lincoln went to school for less than a year, but he loved to read. Later, he studied books on law and became a lawyer.

As a young man, Lincoln worked in a general store in New Salmen, Illinois.

As a young man, Abraham moved to Illinois. He began a career in politics. He worked for the Illinois State government making laws. He was elected to Congress in 1847.

President Abraham Lincoln

In 1861, Abraham Lincoln became the 16th president of the United States. The southern states wanted to break away from the country over the issue of **slavery**. This led to the **Civil War** between the states in the north and the south.

Lincoln gave a speech called the Gettysburg Address during the Civil War.

DID YOU KNOW?

President Lincoln gave a famous speech called the Gettysburg Address. It honored soldiers who died fighting in the Civil War.

In 1863, President Lincoln issued the Emancipation Proclamation, a law that ended slavery in the United States. Some citizens were angry with this law, and he became the first president to be **assassinated**. Shortly before his death in 1865, the states that were against slavery won the Civil War.

● This statue in Boston, Massachusetts, is called "Emancipation." It shows Lincoln freeing a slave.

Presidents' Day Symbols

On Presidents' Day, people use **symbols** to remember presidents. People wave the American flag and dress in red, white, and blue—the colors of the flag.

A famous story about George Washington has become a symbol of his honesty. When he was a boy, George cut down his father's favorite cherry tree to test his new hatchet. Although his father was angry, little George was honest and confessed he had done it.

DID YOU KNOW?

People like to eat cherry pie on Presidents' Day because of Washington's cherry tree story.

President Lincoln often wore a tall, stovepipe hat.

Abraham Lincoln often wore a tall, black hat called a stovepipe hat. It has become a symbol for Lincoln.

How Americans Celebrate

Before the Presidents' Day holiday, many children learn about the presidents of the United States, especially Washington and Lincoln. Some write speeches and do projects.

Children learn about American presidents before Presidents' Day.

DID YOU KNOW?

After he left office, George Washington wrote a Farewell Address. It has been read out loud in the Senate every year for almost 150 years.

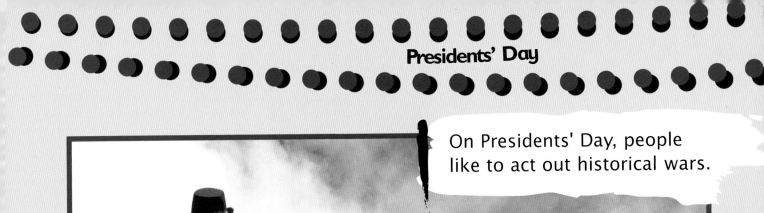

On Presidents' Day, people like to act out historical wars.

Some people go to **wreath**-laying ceremonies, parades, and fireworks displays on Presidents' Day. In some cities people dress in uniforms that look like the ones soldiers wore long ago. They pretend they are fighting in the American Revolution or the Civil War while an audience watches.

During the long weekend, many people go shopping at stores that hold Presidents' Day sales.

Famous Celebrations

The Birthnight Ball is a tradition that was brought to America by British colonists. It was held every year to celebrate the birthday of the **monarch** of England.

Colonists celebrate a Birthnight Ball.

DID YOU KNOW?

In Laredo, Texas, George Washington's birthday is celebrated for one month. Festivities include concerts, fireworks, a parade, air show, and ball.

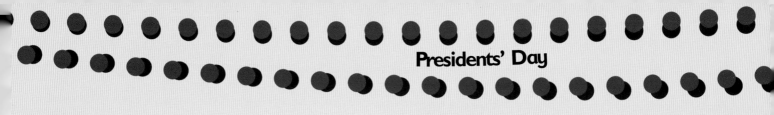

The Gadsby's Tavern holds a Birthnight Ball every year.

When the United States became an independent country, the Birthnight ball was changed to celebrate George Washington's birthday. Washington attended the Birthnight Ball in honor of his birthday at the Gadsby's Tavern in Alexandria, Virginia. This ball is still held today.

Remembering Washington

Americans call George Washington the "Father of our Country" because he was the first president. On Presidents' Day, people visit **memorials** to honor him. A ceremony is also held at George Washington's **tomb** at Mount Vernon on Presidents' Day.

• A picture of George Washington is on the one-dollar bill and the quarter.

DID YOU KNOW?

Many Americans are reminded of George Washington when they see his face on a one-dollar bill or a quarter.

The Washington Monument and the city Washington, D.C. are both named after George Washington.

On Presidents' Day, speeches and a wreath-laying ceremony are held at the Washington Monument in Washington, D.C. It is the largest stone building in the city. It was built in 1885 and stands 555 feet (169 meters) tall.

Remembering Lincoln

Americans honor Abraham Lincoln because he kept the country together during the Civil War and ended slavery. When people visit Washington, D.C., they often go to Ford's Theatre where President Lincoln was assassinated. Today it is a national historic site.

● The penny and five-dollar bill honor President Lincoln.

DID YOU KNOW?

People remember Abraham Lincoln almost every day when they see him on the five-dollar bill and the penny.

This sculpture of Lincoln sits inside the Lincoln Memorial.

The Lincoln Memorial is a building that was built in honor of President Lincoln in the early 1900s. A large sculpture of Lincoln is seated inside. It stands near the Washington Monument in the National Mall, which is a very long park in Washington, D.C. You can see the Lincoln Memorial on the back of the American penny.

Presidential Quiz

1. Who was the first president of the United States of America?
2. When is Presidents' Day celebrated?
3. Who is called the "Father of our Country"?
4. What did Abraham Lincoln do to make America a better country?
5. Where was Abraham Lincoln assassinated?

Presidents Washington, Jefferson, Roosevelt, and Lincoln are carved into Mount Rushmore.

DID YOU KNOW?

The faces of George Washington, Thomas Jefferson, Theodore Roosevelt, and Abraham Lincoln are sculpted into the rock of Mount Rushmore in South Dakota. Each face is 60 feet (18 meters) high.

Answers:
1. George Washington
2. Third Monday in February
3. George Washington
4. Lincoln kept the United States together and helped end slavery
5. Ford's Theatre in Washington, D.C.

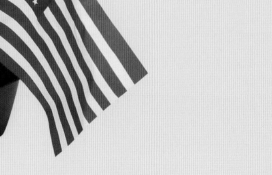

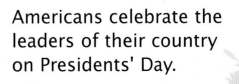

Americans celebrate the leaders of their country on Presidents' Day.

Glossary

assassinate Murder a leader

civil war A war between groups from the same country

colony An area of land that is settled by people who belong to a different country

Congress A group of people elected to make laws

elect To choose by voting

federal Decided by the government

independent A country in charge of its own rules and laws

memorial An object or custom made to help remind you of a person or event

military A group of soldiers prepared to fight

monarch A king or queen who rules over a country

patriotic Love for your country

Senate A group of elected people

slavery Owning and controlling a person, or group of people

surveyor Someone who measures land

symbol An object that stands for something else

tomb A grave

wreath A circle of flowers and leaves

Index

Printed in China—CT